What's A Fraction?

Nancy Kelly Allen

www.rourkepublishing.com

www.rourkepublishing.com

PHOTO CREDITS: Cover: © Darren Fisher, Aleksandr Stennikov; Title Page: © Rosemary Buffoni; Page 3: © gradyreese; Page 4: © Lana Langlois; Page 5: © Kheng Guan Toh; Page 6, 10: © Urs Siedentop; Page 7: © alain cassiede; Page 8, 9: © Denise Kappa; Page 11: © Monkey Business Images; Page 12: © Gustavo Andrade; Page 13, 14, 16, 18, 19: © Picsfive; Page 15: © Oliver Ingrouille; Page 17: © Kai Chiang; Page 20: Leonid Yastremskiy; Page 21: © Darrin Henry; Page 22, 23: © Urs Siedentop, Picsfive;

Edited by Luana Mitten

Cover and Interior design by Teri Intzegian

Library of Congress Cataloging-in-Publication Data

Allen, Nancy Kelly
 What's A Fraction? / Nancy Kelly Allen.
     p. cm. -- (Little World Math)
 Includes bibliographical references and index.
 ISBN 978-1-61741-759-7 (hard cover) (alk. paper)
 ISBN 978-1-61741-961-4 (soft cover)
 Library of Congress Control Number: 2011924806

Rourke Publishing
Printed in the United States of America, North Mankato, Minnesota
060711
060711CL

www.rourkepublishing.com - rourke@rourkepublishing.com
Post Office Box 643328 Vero Beach, Florida 32964

Big share, little share, what is
a fraction?

A fraction is a share of something divided equally.

My pizza is a circle cut into two equal shares called halves.

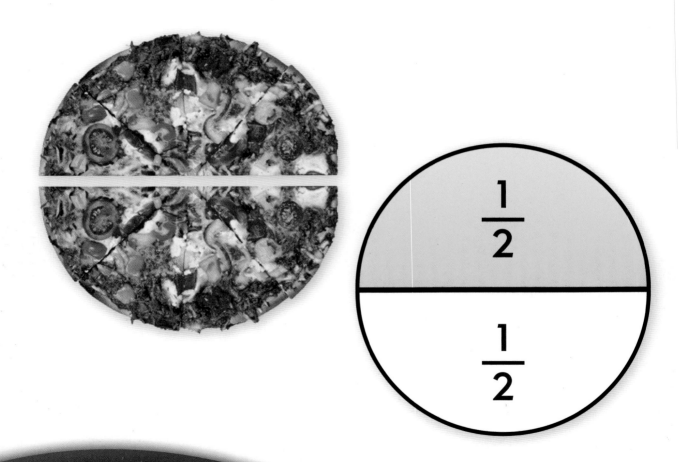

Half of the pizza
is one of the shares.

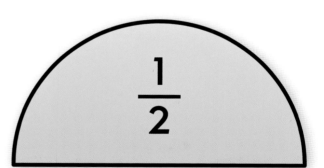

The whole pizza is two shares.

A chocolate bar is a rectangle cut into equal shares. My bar has four shares called quarters or fourths.

A quarter or fourth is one of the shares.

Half is two of the shares.

The whole chocolate bar is four shares.

Let's cut the pizza and chocolate into smaller shares for our friends.

Can you find a fourth, a half, and a whole?

Index

Websites

www.sheppardsoftware.com/mathgames/fractions

www.softschools.com/math/fractions/games

www.aaamath.com/B/g16_frx1.htm#section2

About the Author

Nancy Kelly Allen lives in Kentucky. Half of her house is made of logs. The other half is made of stone. Nancy and her husband, Larry, live in the house with two dogs, Jazi and Roxi. The two dogs claim more than half their share of space.